FIGHTBACK
from a Brain Tumour

One family's account of living with a brain tumour

Jason Oliver

Images: Jason Oliver & Kirsty Oliver
Editing: Rachael Oliver
Proofreading: Rachael Oliver & Nico Dattani
Cover design: Graeme Fayers

Official website: http://fightback-from-a-brain-tumour.com/

Contents

Foreword

My name is Rachael (Rache), Jason's wife of 24 years at the time of writing.

We got married in 1996 after a four-year engagement and had two children in 2000 and 2002 respectively.

Life was good, two new babies, building dreams and hopes for the future, then on the second January 2004, our path changed quite dramatically when Jason was rushed into hospital and that is where our new normal begins.

A whole new world opened up to us, we were not familiar with hospitals at all, let alone Addenbrooke's. Up to this point, I had not even driven to Cambridge before.

Unaware of the events that were to unfold; from having the initial shock to still having scan anxiety today (into our mid to late forties), it never leaves us. Dealing with this trauma at just 28 and 30 years old when our family life was just beginning was horrific, a time we would never get back.

Our inner strength took over - more like autopilot kicked in and we just had to go along with it; sink or swim. We could not change it but over the years we learned how to accept it in our day to day lives and dance in the rain.

There were times when we felt we were drowning but this episode has certainly enriched our lives in many ways. We found that we certainly were not alone in this and others in this world do go through traumatic events as well, why should we be any different? We consider ourselves blessed with the outcomes we have had. Yes, our lives have been clouded by it, but feel extremely grateful as the implications could have been so much worse.

Jason is a strong, caring, loving man and is the bravest person I know. He never showed us that he was scared although we all felt it. His strength and positivity throughout helped us to be strong and positive. But do not be misled, we did have our wobbles, it is only natural, and we are only human.

If you or someone close to you has been diagnosed with a brain tumour, I am sure you will benefit from reading Jason's story. Although this is a true account of what happened in our lives, your journey may differ, but you will likely have similar doubts and fears to manage as we did. Although Jason's risk is lower now, it is always there in the back of our minds.

Remember you are not alone; you will find your way of dealing with it, and I just hope this book is of comfort and support to you, as intended.

Preface

Almost 11,700 people, diagnosed each year with a primary brain tumour, including 500 children and young people – that is *32 people every day*.

This book, the first I have written, is not intended as an autobiography but as a digestible excerpt.

I feel incredibly fortunate to have come through this fight and have borne my heart and soul in this book. My sole motivation for sharing my encounter is in the hope it will help comfort and inspire others following a similar path.

Dedication

This book is dedicated to all the health professionals who have helped me through this period and ultimately saved my life; I have tried to call out the many individuals and teams throughout the chapters. Until the COVID-19 pandemic in 2020, not enough praise was given to NHS staff, who are, in my opinion, the lifeblood of this great nation.

Also, this book is dedicated to those special people in my life who planted the strength in me that I needed, when I did not even realise that I had it, and to all those around me who have been my rock, and also, to those who have tolerated my changes and frustrations.

A special dedication goes to my family, especially my lovely wife and children, for the impact this saga has had on their lives, robbing them of their years and childhood. I am so very proud of the way my wife, children, and parents have coped and stepped up to the challenge throughout this ordeal. It is not something that they asked for, but dealt with it all, unconditionally. I could not have done it without them.

Thank you.

Prologue

My name is Jason Oliver. A typical middle-aged man and husband to a beautiful wife for over two decades and a dedicated father to a wonderful son and daughter. We were blessed with a child of each gender and consider ourselves a close and caring family with good support from our large extended families, along with great friends.

Me and my family in October 2003.

I am passionate about sports cars and creating digital music; my dream life would have been to be either a successful music producer or a racing car driver. I also enjoy photography and travelling.

I am not what you would call a sporty person, being somewhat chubby most of my life. Despite my physical presence, I was often bullied at school, predominately as I managed to become the adversary of the popular kid at school.

With my Mum's help, through dieting and jogging, I managed to lose some childhood *puppy fat*! I carried on this trend and hit the gym when I left school to replace fat with muscle. Shortly after this, I attended my first Karate class, and something in me just clicked - luckily, no bones - I had found my *thing*. I stuck to regular training throughout my life, progressing through belts and tournaments, except for about five years while our children were little.

My job is a cloud architect, meaning that I am responsible for constructing innovative IT systems and have been progressing to this point my whole life. I have been privileged to have worked for and alongside the best in my time, with lots of international travel, and worked on some prestigious projects, highlights include supporting the IT systems of a Formula One team at the factory and trackside.

Fridge Magnet

At some point in my early thirties, I remember being gifted with a fridge magnet similar to that illustrated below.

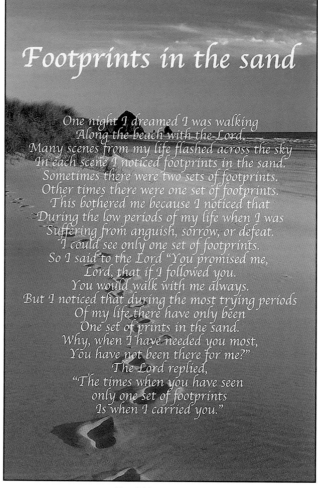

One night I dreamed I was walking
Along the beach with the Lord.
Many scenes from my life flashed across the sky
In each scene I noticed footprints in the sand.
Sometimes there were two sets of footprints.
Other times there were one set of footprints.
This bothered me because I noticed that
During the low periods of my life when I was
Suffering from anguish, sorrow, or defeat.
I could see only one set of footprints.
So I said to the Lord "You promised me,
Lord, that if I followed you.
You would walk with me always.
But I noticed that during the most trying periods
Of my life there have only been
One set of prints in the sand.
Why, when I have needed you most,
You have not been there for me?"
The Lord replied,
"The times when you have seen
only one set of footprints
Is when I carried you."

The fridge magnet.

I recall thinking what a load of *old guff,* as I could not relate to the words. I was not from what you would call a devoted Christian family, although I had attended Sunday school as a child, and do consider myself a believer.

Despite my poor lifestyle choices, I was always a healthy man and boy alike. I did start to lose my hair at the age of fourteen, which was tough, especially for a chubby lad at school. However, before I turned the age of thirty in November 2003, I rarely suffered any health issues whatsoever; I barely caught a cold and cannot recall having the flu until into my thirties!

This was all set to change...

Blue Lights

The two weeks leading up to Christmas 2003, I suffered headaches, not memorably bad headaches, but odd nonetheless, since I rarely suffered from headaches. In hindsight, I wish I had listened to and trusted in what my body was telling me. I was taking paracetamol and ibuprofen like Smarties, and they did not seem to be helping; eventually, the pain was severe enough for me to consult a general practitioner (GP). I told him I had numbness around my mouth.

The GP did not think there was anything wrong, so sent me on my way with the advice to return the first week of January when they could carry out a blood test. I continued to suffer in silence throughout the festive season with no idea what was to come next.

On the second of January 2004, I woke to the most painful headache you could ever imagine, this combined with the feeling of dizziness and nausea with ice-cold sweats, I knew something was wrong.

Rache awoke to see me gazing out of the bedroom window and asked if I was okay, before I darted to the toilet to vomit. She instinctively reached out to call an ambulance. However, I resisted saying it was nothing and would likely soon pass; for all I knew it might have been related to earlier New Year's celebrations. *Why is it that we are dismissive of our instincts and so reluctant to call upon our public health services?*

Rache insisted to call 111 if not 999, who advised us to go straight to our nearest accident and emergency hospital.

Rache stayed at home with our two young children while my dad drove me to our local hospital. Fortunately, my dad lived in the same town, so was with us in no time, despite this all happening early in the morning.

The 15-mile journey seemed to take an age on this Friday morning, and I continued to vomit into a makeshift sick bag for most of the journey, still experiencing piercing headaches and cold sweats. I cannot imagine how my dad remained focused on driving.

It was my first time in a hospital as a patient since stitching up a small hand-wound as a teenager.

On arrival, my dad sought for the medical team to prioritise me ahead of all the seasonally intoxicated, and I was immediately given something for the pain; this was a much-appreciated respite after experiencing the pain for many hours now.

After being taken to a private bay for the usual tests, blood samples, etc., we were advised they had booked me in for a computerized axial tomography (CAT) scan. I remember, my dad and I were left alone in the bay pondering this new development for some time with anxious minds; quietly we both feared the worst but remained upbeat and positive trying not to let the fear in, or admit the truth of the situation to ourselves or each other, it was a bizarre emotional standoff.

The moment was broken when I got wheeled off for my CAT scan. My inner geek immediately awoke, and I was more in awe of the engineering than scared when I saw the machine. I laid down and was momentarily consumed by this humming white cylinder. This was followed by more waiting with my dad before we were presented with their findings, that we had been quietly dreading.

We were told that I had a *mass* inside my head. Besides this, they offered little in the way of an explanation, informing us they were going to move me to the centre of excellence for this type of thing.

They told us that I would be transported by Ambulance under blue flashing lights. I am certain the only reason for this was compensation to soften the blow of such traumatic news, as there appeared to be little urgency from that point onwards. Luckily, in the build-up to this moment, my dad and I had psyched ourselves up for this, so it was not as impacting as it perhaps should have been.

My dad had somehow found the courage to drive back from the hospital alone. By that time Rache and kids were sat waiting with my Mum and Nan, my Nan was by chance visiting over the festive period. They had all been together since lunchtime expectantly waiting for an update.

Dad appeared at the door late afternoon and he updated the family with the tragic news. It was such a shock to them all. Rache remembers feeling like her stomach had dropped out and just shook, her legs turned to jelly.

I cannot dare to imagine what they were all going through, through all lenses, as my spouse, my parents, my grandparent, and my children.

For me, the ambulance distraction had worked; I enjoyed my thrilling ride and was like a big kid at a theme park! I was having banter with the crew about their driving. They talked me through the special vehicle, procedures they had for driving through speed cameras, and their day-to-day experiences. I was fascinated and almost forgot why I was there! All too soon, we arrived.

I want to thank the accident and emergency department at Ipswich Hospital for their quick and thorough triaging of my case, and the Ambulance crew for keeping my spirits high at this volatile time.

Addenbrooke's

When we arrived, I remember thinking what a massive site Addenbrooke's was, with lots of staff and patients all over the place. It is a departure from the local hospital I was familiar with up until this point.

My dad drove Rache to Addenbrooke's to meet me. Rache was beside herself with emotion, which I struggled to deal with as by that time, I had learnt to accept my fate, so was puzzled why she had not. She was working on a compressed timeline and playing catchup with the developments.

At the time, my son and daughter would have been just three and one years old respectively; I did not see them earlier that morning as they were asleep when all the commotion broke. In the meantime, they had been taken to Rache's parents so that Rache had the flexibility to be with me for the duration without having to worry about their care too.

I was taken for a more detailed magnetic resonance imaging (MRI) scan. The MRI scanner is a long white cylindrical device, like a large pack of polo mints with a sliding bed. I was immersed head-first into the cylindrical device with my head secured into a position to keep it still. Then scanned for several fifteen to twenty-minute sessions separated by an injection of a medical dye to enhance the imagery.

The scanner was noisy; earplugs were provided, but despite this, I could still hear the clicking, buzzing, and whirring for the duration.

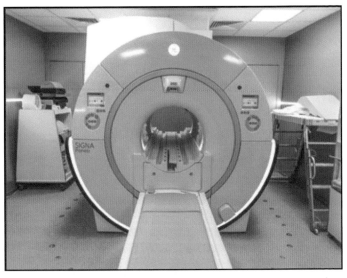
A typical MRI scanner.

The specialists eventually shared my diagnosis and told us that I had a tumour to the right side of my brain. We were all devastated but quick to accept the truth; we were almost anticipating it by this point.

The most significant two questions I asked at the time were why me, and what caused this? Both massive questions that I had an uncontrollable thirst for answers to. Neither questions have been answered to this day.

At the time, I knew little about what a brain tumour was, and had only ever heard of one case previously; Rache's aunty who unexpectedly died with a brain stem tumour in 1996. My news resonated with Rache and brought back all the memories and raw emotions of this, and naturally, she was terrified.

I was given steroids to reduce the pressure the tumour was applying inside my skull, this also helped ease the pain, although I am sure having the confidence of being located in the centre of excellence at Addenbrooke's helped with this comfort. All the staff were caring and highly skilled; for the first time, I felt a sense of relief.

A nurse asked why we had not spotted the increased size and shape of my head, which in hindsight, I can see from old photographs but growing little-by-little over the years it had gone unnoticed. We started to question how long it was in there for, and whether me losing my hair at such a young age was a sign.

We were told that I could not be operated on for a few days as they had to wait for the swelling to go down. I stayed in for observation, securing a bed, and awaiting an operation slot.

I remember laying in my bed waiting for the day of the operation was tough; I lay there alone once visiting hours were over with too much time to contemplate.

Rache had brought our children in to see me on Sunday, and we had the opportunity to have lunch like a normal family in the hospital food court. I doted on my children and would ordinarily be going stir-crazy not seeing them for this long. I wondered what must have been going through their little minds as I knew they were compassionate and caring beyond their years. This must have been a harrowing experience for them as they saw first-hand, people including young children being wheeled around with bandages, and connected to drips.

On the day before the operation, a small posse came to visit us to explain the procedure. We were advised that I would need to surrender my driving licence for the foreseeable future.

They gave me a consent form to read and sign; this explained that there was a small risk to me being killed or being mentally and/or physically disabled for the rest of my life. I remember thinking who in their right mind would sign such a thing, but of course, there was no choice, and I had to put my faith and life in their hands.

Everyone goes through the situation, but in the ward, when the light goes out, it is just you who faces it alone.

Wednesday arrived, just five days on from waking with the symptoms, it was the day of the operation. It was an early start, Rache and my parents came to Addenbrooke's to see me before I went up to the operating theatre. I was first on the list that day.

Rache came up in the lift with the nurse and porters so she could see where I was going to be, we said our goodbyes and good lucks then the porter took her back down to meet my Mum and Dad. They had plans to go into Cambridge shopping to try to take their minds off the operation while remaining nearby.

I came-too about eight hours later with my head in agony. I was restrained to the bed, with drains coming from my head and bandages covering my head. Disoriented from the anaesthetic, it was all a shock to me.

Fortunately, I had a lovely nurse by my side, who calmly eased me back into consciousness. I recall she said that because of my build, I had had enough Morphine to subdue a fully-grown deer! I was not quite sure whether this was a good or bad thing, but it did comfort me at the time.

Back at the ward, I was elated to see Rache and my parents. A brief tear came to my eyes before I wrestled it back again. I had made it; I had come out on the other side.

Rache burst into tears with overwhelming emotion at the shock of seeing me like this, and one of the nurses hugged and reassured her.

The day after, I remember looking at my yellow-coloured self in the ward's toilet mirror; by then, my bandages had been removed, to unveil a massive horseshoe-shaped scar with staples along its length on the side of my misshaped head.

The specialists told us that they had successfully removed a grade II meningioma tumour of 15cm x 3-4cm x 3-4cm in size, approximately a typical TV remote controller but deeper, which was removed in two pieces. I wondered how there was room for that inside my skull!

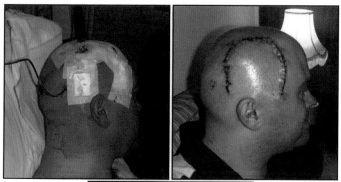

Me immediately after my first operation and back at home.

I knew then that my world had changed forever. I spent the rest of that morning crying into my pillow, surrounded by strangers. I was concerned about Rache and my family seeing my new form. Many hours later, the registrar visited me to console me. I had never cried so many tears in my life and hoped not to again. I guess I needed a release after keeping it all bottled up for so many days.

I was told that I would be monitored through regular MRI scans at Addenbrooke's to check for any further growths.

I want to thank Mr Waters and his team and all the nurses and staff on A-ward at Addenbrooke's Hospital for their indispensable talent and care, and for saving my life. Words cannot do them justice.

The Mask

Knowing I was fixed, I was keen to get out of the hospital as quickly as possible, not through lack of care, in fact the opposite. I felt reassured and at peace in the well-being of the first-class care I was provided at Addenbrooke's. However, I was missing my family, home routine, and normality.

Astonishingly, through my determination and the support of my family, I was discharged just two days after such a major operation.

While we all felt a little anxious about me being outside the bubble of professional health care, I did feel great recovering at home surrounded by my family, home comforts, and the freedom to do as I pleased at any time of day.

After the operation, I recall feeling the sensation of fluids rushing in my head, the consultant told us that this was due to the healing process and everything settling down. Also, I found it painful to have any build-up of pressure in my head, so struggled with bending down, sneezing, etc. I particularly remember smelling of Morphine for weeks, as my dose was very high.

Such a significant health concern puts things into perspective, and I promised myself that I would improve my lifestyle. Looking back on things, I can genuinely say that this was the catalyst that began a course-correction on my life. Albeit not the instant and far-reaching change I had envisaged.

I was keen to bounce back as it was my son's fourth birthday just ten days after I was discharged. I was adamant to visit our local toy store to help pick out my son's present, his first Scalextric set – a rite of passage for any father-son relationship, so I was grateful to be able to do this.

Despite having a supportive employer, I found myself back at work just two months later, building up from light duties. I felt driven to prove to myself and others that I could be normal again and missed fulfilling a role and purpose. I recall taking a difficult vocational exam shortly after just to prove myself mentally capable, and soon returned to Karate, albeit in a teaching capacity.

On my return to work, my employer and colleagues presented us with an astounding £800-worth of holiday vouchers so that we could take a much-needed family holiday. We were blown away by this generosity.

We went to a holiday park in Poole with this wonderful gift, where we had a lot of fun and shared laughs, with the occasional emotive tear at the realisation of what we had been through, and how lucky we were to have this lovely holiday.

I was regularly monitored, with a combination of an MRI scan, that I had now forced myself to enjoy the unnatural experience of, followed by a face-to-face consultation both taking place over multiple days in Cambridge.

This felt reassuring, as while it was an inconvenience, I knew others could be walking through life with a similar illness completely unaware, and without any such support - I was in a privileged position to be under this care.

Later in May the same year, just a few months following the operation, I was called back to Addenbrooke's as there were signs of residual cells that were typical of this type of tumour. It was a risk we had accepted and hoped we would never have to face. It was disturbing news, as we feared that we have to go through more surgery. However, instead, we agreed on a course of lesser invasive radiotherapy.

Radiotherapy is a therapy using ionizing radiation, to control or kill malignant cells and normally delivered by a linear accelerator, a massive space-like device in the middle of its capacious dedicated room.

Before therapy could begin, a bespoke mask had to be produced to ensure my head could be locked down during the treatment to maintain accuracy.

The mask construction required me to lay down whilst warm plaster of Paris was applied to my head in strips, leaving small slits for my eyes, nose, and mouth. Once set, they made an acrylic mould from this. Rache sat with me throughout the half-day procedure and was horrified at what I had to endure, yet somehow, I was unfazed by the process and simply let them get on with their job knowing it would soon be over.

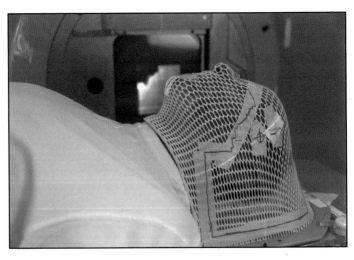

An updated variation of my radiotherapy mask.

For the radiotherapy alone, I had to rely on others to ferry me on the 2+ hour, 100-mile round trip, at the same time, every day, five times a week, week-in-week-out for six weeks.

Again, my wife, extended family, and our employers were incredibly supportive. And again, the hospital staff were kind and put my mind at rest, always keeping spirits high. However, the treatment left me feeling incredibly lethargic for the remainder of the day, no matter how hard I tried to fight it, I was good for nothing else.

The process left my already balding scalp without hair on both sides of my head where the beam had passed through. To minimise the impact this has on me, I try and keep to a short haircut, which opposes Rache's preference. This only seems to pull focus to the side of my head where the scar from the operation is evident.

At this time, I was also undergoing speech therapy to help, as the operation had damaged my jaw muscles, and I found it difficult to open my mouth to its normal extent and pronounce my words.

Once my six-week treatment plan had ended, we reset, and all felt hopeful for a positive future again.

This was all great, but I was still heavily reliant upon Rache and family for my independence until I received my driving licence back again, as the radiotherapy extended my licence revocation by a year.

With this all behind us, we did have some good times, actually some great times. In 2006, we had our first family holiday abroad; we went to a child-friendly resort in Majorca where we all enjoyed the rest, relaxation, and fun that we all deserved. It was so good that we pushed the boat out and went back to the same place the following year! I feel that this helped heal our combined psyche while building my confidence back.

I started driving again around September 2005. My son started playing with a football team, and my daughter started dance classes. The equilibrium of life was returning.

Sadly, in 2008, I was made redundant. However, I was quickly head-hunted to work in the prestigious world of Formula One, where I supported a team with their IT systems in the factory and even trackside during their final race in Barcelona. For a motor racing fan, this was a dream job that gave me many fond memories.

Me on the at Circuit de Barcelona-Catalunya.

I want to thank the oncology department at Addenbrooke's Hospital for their expertise and care.

Dark Times

I cannot recall when, but I learned that the radiotherapy had not been successful, and there was possibly another *growth* and that Addenbrooke's would keep an eye on it.

I felt that I could not share this with *anyone*, wanting to protect them from further suffering, and give them as much time to live a life without further impact and pain as possible.

Of all the times, on Christmas Eve 2008, we had a call from Addenbrooke's to confirm that I did indeed have another tumour, it was decided it could be left for now, as it was small. However, it did not stop us from worrying like crazy, preoccupying our thoughts over the festive period, and kept pondering when it should be removed for a few months afterwards.

As the breadwinner of the household, this decision was primarily influenced by my employer, who was far less generous and supportive than the previous one. Also, because we understood the inevitability of the situation and that my employer would only pay the basic statutory sick pay of just £80 per week, we started tightening our belt to *save* for the event.

We had to cut back on our son's birthday, and we were even unable to afford my daughter's preferred birthday present of Sylvanian Families figures, which as a proud dad, broke my heart beyond words – even to this day. We could not even treat our family to indulgences while shopping – something we had taken for granted; this made me well up in the supermarket.

We called our local Citizens Advice for advice and tried our bank to get a mortgage holiday, but they wanted an admin fee to do that, which we just could not afford on the bread line. We remember breaking down outside the bank.

We tried the council, but the form they sent was vast, and any help means-tested. We sold Rache's car to help with the bills, and luckily, we had some savings for modest home improvements that helped us a bit too. These were *dark times*, and for the first time, I was struggling to cope.

By chance, my Mum put us in touch with a local charity through a friend, who kindly donated £100 to us and £25 to each of the children. This kind gesture helped lifted our spirits, and our children wrote a charming thank you letter back.

Adding insult to injury, in April 2009, I experienced my first seizure. I was lying in bed, and all of a sudden,

I started making strange noises, bleeding from and foaming up at the mouth, and jolted myself out of bed. Rache immediately called the emergency services as she had never seen anything like this before. By this time, I was unconscious, my foot was trapped behind the radiator, and my head was under the bed!

Rache thought the worst as I was not breathing, and she cried out to the emergency operator that she had lost me! Calmly, the operator instructed Rache to listen to my breathing and to put me in the recovery position. Then she mentioned that I would need to pass fluids once I had come around. I then gasped, woke, and went to the toilet.

By this time, my eight-year-old son had helped Rache by welcoming the paramedics into the house. Confused, I walked out of the toilet and saw two strange men in uniform in our bedroom and asked them what they were doing in my house! They observed the situation and left shortly afterwards. It transpired I had suffered a tonic-clonic seizure.

This episode left Rache feeling highly anxious about my health. She watched me sleep for many weeks later, and was on edge should I have another seizure again at any time and anywhere. She was a wreck through worry.

Having a seizure required me to surrender my driving licence once again for another year.

A month later, I had a smaller seizure, I recall feeling dizzy and that the room was darkening, collapsing in on me. While still scary, this time we were all wiser, and thankfully managed the situation on our own.

Meeting with the consultant, we decided that I should opt for the surgery in the hope that it would prevent further seizures. I was told that this would be a smaller, less intrusive operation.

Just a month later, I had my second resection operation to remove the new troublesome growth. I had to sign the same consent form as before, but the consultant warned us that I could potentially have a seizure during the operation. The thought of this scared us and consumed Rache's thoughts. She was comforted to have her Mum there as well as my parents while I was undergoing the operation.

It was an emotional send-off, on the way to the operating theatre I said to Rache that it would be just *a walk in the park*, I have no idea where those words came from, but it was an attempt to reassure us both, nonetheless. Again, I was trying to fight to expose my true fear that I was feeling inside. I felt I had to be strong to help those around me cope; I felt guilty as nobody had signed up for any of this tragedy. The doors of the lift closed, shutting off our loving gaze. I was now completely alone.

The surgeon went in at the point of my first resection to reduce the impact of the surgery, then veered off about 6 centimetres at an angle towards the frontal lobe to access the new growth. Fortunately, I did not have a seizure during the operation, so this was a huge relief to all concerned.

Coming around afterwards, I did not feel too bad, although I remember having the sensation of marbles rolling around in my head. Luckily, I did not have such a high dose of Morphine as I had in my first operation, so I felt good.

Later that day, I had banter with the surgeon about joining him at the gym the following morning as I felt so good after the operation, the ward started joining in saying they would also be there with us!

Luckily, this operation caused no real drama in terms of recovery or impact on my life. I bounced back and returned to work in no time. This was needed as by this time; our savings were used up and we were heavily into our overdraft, with the bank declining further funds.

The following month, I had another bout of seizures. I woke Rache as I knew I was not feeling well; she brought me downstairs and gave me some water. It developed into a serious episode.

I was in and out of multiple seizures. Rache rung the emergency services straight away followed by my Mum and Dad. By this time the children were awake, and she needed help.

When the paramedics arrived, they observed several more seizures then when they believed I was stable they put me on a stretcher, and we left in the ambulance to West Suffolk Hospital.

Rache had to sit in the front of the ambulance with the paramedic, for her safety. He reassured her that he was familiar with seizures. I suffered another seizure en route, so they had to pull into a layby to attend to me. We eventually arrived at the hospital where they heavily sedated me, and I stayed in all weekend.

I recall waking up alone, dressed in a gown, on a bed in a hospital corridor, with no comprehension of how I got there. Nobody seemed to come near-or-by for hours or what felt like days; I was disorientated and alone...and pretty frightened. It was the kind of experience you expect to see in a horror movie.

I cannot convey in words the sense of relief and love I had when I finally saw Rache walk towards me from a distance. I was later told that I was alone for a matter of minutes, but this goes to illustrate the impact the incident and medication had on me.

This event was disappointing as we were led to believe the seizures were caused by the tumour, which had now been removed. This put doubt in our minds that there may be further tumours.

At our next appointment with the consultant at Addenbrooke's, we were notified that there were no more tumours, *a huge relief*! The seizures were caused by internal scarring from my operations. I was then prescribed anti-seizure medication, which would prevent any further occurrences.

I tried to block the nagging what-ifs from my mind, but I felt exhausted and knew there was *NO WAY* that I could face another operation. I shared this with my family, as I knew they felt the same way. We all had faith, so knew this would not be an issue. *We were over this*.

I want to thank Mr Price and his team and all the nurses and staff on A-ward at Addenbrooke's Hospital for their indispensable talent and care, and for saving my life. Words cannot do them justice. I would also like to thank West Suffolk Hospital, the paramedics (especially Steven Nunn), for their help and reassurance, and the 999-service operator for her calming influence.

Done

Done, or so we thought! I was now working a high-profile job in London, having changed my job to one commutable on the rail network as my driving licence was still revoked.

Working hard and playing just as hard. I enjoyed the autonomy my job gave me and working with a great team around me.

We started recovering financially. These were good times while still being monitored by Addenbrooke's. Life was finally returning to normal.

However, in May 2011, results from my latest scan showed two further growths, and we were informed that I required a significant operation to remove them. I cannot tell you how deep our hearts sank at this news.

While I had managed to keep upbeat through the saga up to this point, I genuinely felt physically and mentally defeated and that I could not go on with this continued onslaught. I remember thinking if this is it, then so be it. I would be ok with that. I no longer had any fight left in me. I had accepted my fate; this would be the end of my journey.

Rache burst into tears and could not believe the news we had just been told. We thought we were on the up, I did not have any symptoms, and the seizures were being managed by the medication. It was a bolt out of the blue, and we just were not expecting this.

This is where the Lord met me at my point of need. I was in the darkest of dark places; I had lost all sign of hope and faith which disgusted me even more. Our church was sympathetic and supportive, offering condolence and group prayer. I recall that I immersed myself in faith – this is all I had to fight my final fight, there was no plan b, no backstop.

Besides regularly attending the Sunday service, I attended as many extra prayer sessions as I could. Rache and I would read the bible at night and pray as though our lives depended on it. *We were desperate*.

I recall that throughout all the prayers, one prayer amongst all others hit me like a thunderbolt. I felt something inside me change then and there. I pinned all my hopes on this one spiritual encounter; it empowered me to move on and face whatever was to come next.

I received a letter informing me of the scheduled date so braced myself for the operation only to get a call saying this had been postponed for four days later. I cannot tell you how disheartened I was, given the energy I had invested in preparing for this.

Devastatingly and unexpectedly, Rache's Nan passed away on the day the operation was originally scheduled. She was very close to her Nan and found this whole situation emotionally overwhelming.

The morning of my operation came, I called Rache and spoke to my children, which was probably the hardest thing I have ever had to do; on the one hand, I had to manage my own emotions talking to my young family realising that it may be the last time I do so, and, on the other, I had to be strong for them knowing that I could not let any of my feelings surface to add to their fears and anxieties.

I waited for my operation on a bed in the operating theatre of all places, not a prep room I was accustomed to. The room was filled with what looked to be high-tech variants of specialised DIY tools that hung around the walls of the room. It resembled some ultra-sterile engineers shed as much as an operating theatre.

I was talking to my surgeon before the operation, trying to quickly build a rapport with the man who held my future in his hands. It became apparent that there were four tumours in my head, not the two I had been advised of as recently as that morning. This put me in a dilemma; I wanted to be sure he was working from the right notes but wanted to be sure he was not going to perform undue surgery, without patronising the man who would be performing my resection in moments. It would not be the first time I have had my records mixed up in a hospital!

When I had recovered from the surgery, I was told that they had to *cut my head in half* to enable access and ensure they could remove all four tumours and surrounding cells. I remember paraphrasing my prognosis to my family, telling them that I was *riddled with the things*!

While we were waiting for further news, it quickly became obvious this was a more significant operation than I had experienced before, when I realised that I had lost control of my left hand. Initially, I was unable to even clench my fist or move my fingers; this was a terrifying discovery.

Despite that, I was adamant about discharging myself as quickly as possible to pay my respects and support Rache and the family at her Nan's funeral, this was the least I could do after everything I had put them through.

I attended rehabilitation for a while to help retrain my brain how to use the fine-motor controls on my left hand. My left arm would often feel like a heavy meat joint swinging from my shoulder. Around two weeks later, I could hold an object in both hands at the same time; this was great progress.

In January 2012, through consultation with my GP and Addenbrooke's Hospital, it was agreed that we would explore weaning me off my anti-seizure medication, since any tablet has side effects, and it would be good to get me off this lifelong dependency – especially given my borderline need for the medication, as I was prescribed a low dose. It was agreed the timing would be ideal since I was already off the road due to my operation the previous May.

Regretfully, the experiment did not pay off. When the drug had fully depleted from my system, it sparked another seizure whilst I was working in London. It was a hot day in July; I was chairing an important assembly in an underground meeting room with ten people in attendance from multiple organisations.

I recall feeling strange, so without saying anything, slowly eased myself to sit on the floor. However, I am not sure I declared how I felt until the very last minute through the feeling of utter embarrassment and shame.

The next thing I know, the paramedics had arrived, and I was being stretchered out of the building into an ambulance parked outside the office in the narrow street. Many colleagues passed me returning from their lunch break, which was an incredibly humbling moment of my life.

My parents drove the two hundred mile round-trip with Rache to pick me up from the London-based hospital where I was eventually discharged that same, long hot day. My boss kindly sat with me until they arrived.

I was immediately put back on my anti-seizure medication, *this time for life*, as I could no longer afford to surrender my driving licence through health conditions.

This was an unfortunate blip which needed to be tested. However, I was back at work the following day to face the music. Fortunately, everyone was kind not to draw attention to my incident.

With regular MRI scans taking place, Addenbrooke's, sensitive to my long commute to the hospital, kindly developed a telephone clinic service, piloting the service on me. This was touted a huge success, and the nurse responsible rightly received an accolade for her work on this, and we were both quoted in a local newspaper endorsing this then-innovative approach to medical health consultation.

I want to thank Mr Watts and his team (especially Ingela Oberg) and all the nurses and staff on A-ward at Addenbrooke's Hospital for their indispensable talent and care, and for saving my life. Words cannot do them justice. I would also like to thank the paramedics and staff at the Royal London Hospital.

Hope

Every good story should have a happy ever after, and I am pleased to say that mine is no different.

The following year I came out of my high-pressured role in London to settle into a more sedate pace with a local role. This came at a price as I halved my salary overnight which brought about new pressures and knocked my confidence.

Every operation and seizure put me off the road for another 12+ months meaning that in all, I was off the road for most of an entire decade! This was agonising for someone who enjoys both their independence and driving.

After car sharing with a friend from Karate for almost a year, I eventually got my driving licence back. The moment I could drive I managed to get a convertible for the commute. This is something I had on my bucket list, my family all clubbed together and helped me purchase it for my fortieth birthday and restored some much-needed independence.

Shortly afterwards, I managed to find a new job paying a more realistic salary, with a boss who believed in me and stretched my career ambitions. With his help, I restored some lost confidence, and he helped me on my professional trajectory.

The opportunity arose for me to upgrade to an actual sports car – nothing flash but something fun and impractical, nonetheless. This was a seminal moment for me as when I was ten years old, my dad prophesied that I would own a sports car one day – showing his confidence in me, so I was honoured to be able to fulfil his foresight thirty years on, and still enjoy this car today.

I am used to changing jobs to further my career, and despite my *disability*, have managed to go from strength-to-strength. I am now working for a decent company with an acceptable commute; it is nice to work and live in the same county and is something I had been missing for many years.

I continue to test my mental capability by stretching myself in my career, and third-party recognition through passing top-tier industry assessments. I feel that I have finally found my niche and am becoming a leader in my field.

During my ordeals, my Karate sensei helped me by making me mentally and physically tough to face these situations. Back in 2006, I was physically fit and in training for my black belt. Sadly, after the second and third operations, with all the mental and physical setbacks, in addition to the sands of time, I felt like that ship had sailed.

The phrase *fightback* came to me when I turned forty, and I was determined to give it my all with Karate to achieve my goal. I trained three to four nights a week, again at the weekend and two to three times a week, first thing in the mornings in the gym.

On the back of a gruelling outdoor summer camp, in August 2018 (the hottest summer on record for England), in a building with the thermal properties of a greenhouse, I climbed my summit and attained my black belt at one of the nation's premier clubs, a significant event for me that I had been working towards for over 25 years!

I now enjoy teaching others to give back to the sport and the community, and grateful that my recovery has enabled me to complete my journey.

I want to thank my good friend, sensei, and life coach, Halstead Ottley, for his patience and support in helping me achieve my black belt in Karate, and become the person I am today.

Me with my sensei, Halstead Ottley, after receiving my black belt.

I am passionate about helping those who are bullied, and if I won the lottery, I would like to start-up and run a charity and offer coaching and self-defence classes to help eradicate this.

Meanwhile, my regular check-ups are now stretched out to every two years, so onward and upwards. I have now had seven consecutive all-clears in the last six years. While this is not technically *remission,* as my tumour is not classified as cancer, it does mean that my chance of future growths is about the same as anyone else.

This may all seem like I have been left without any negative impact on my life; this is not the case. I feel I am running at one hundred miles per hour just to keep up to look like I am walking at a normal pace - this can be exhausting but something I must do to survive.

My issues are predominantly caused by my last operation, leaving my left-hand with limited tactile feedback, meaning that I am no longer able to open a plastic bag or play the piano and struggle to touch type like I once did.

Also, cosmetically, my head has been left distorted and no longer symmetrical, which would usually not be a problem; however, when you are a follicly-challenged man, this is a problem. This is an issue for my confidence in my career, client meetings, networking events, and even talking at International conferences, and I find this disability has held me back on all counts. I still live with limited jaw movement to this day, which is more of an issue for my dentist than it is to me!

I once heard that scars are the wounds of war...and I should consider myself to have won the war! This is a unique spin on things!

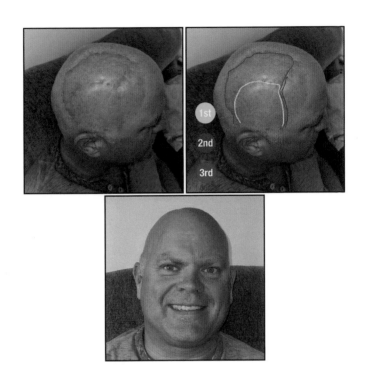

Me now the scars from all three operations.

I mentioned earlier that my two biggest questions were, why me, and what caused this? And that neither questions have been answered to this day.

I started to look at implementing a technical solution to address this a few years ago. With no medical expertise, I thought of designing a simple online survey for patients to share lifestyle details. Then using big data solutions to identify any trends that may point towards a potential cause that everyone could avoid. Sadly, this idea did not get off the ground.

I was recently honoured to become a BRIAN champion volunteering for the Brain Tumour Charity. BRIAN is an online app that has been developed by The Brain Tumour Charity to help people cope with a brain tumour. BRIAN will help you - and those supporting you - to understand how you are doing and to make better-informed decisions. I am hoping it will provide insights such as those I was seeking and has a lot of synergy with my original vision.

Throughout the whole saga, I have been fortunate enough, through the skill of the medical services and dedicated professionals, to continue a normal life with my family, friends, and work colleagues. It is not the same normal as before – but *a new normal*.

This is not to be understated, given the severity of surgery and risks associated, it is outstanding and something I should never be complacent about, it is a miracle.

Of course, there are times when I am reminded of the ordeal, and I break down; I think this is only natural, and part of the healing process. Hearing any similar account sets me off as does random movies, and I mean random...it could even be a Disney animation!

On reflection, I now understand the meaning of that fridge magnet. Despite people praising my heroics of getting through this ordeal, I did not; I believe it was the Lord carrying me through the situation while I lay asleep at peace.

If you or someone you know is following a similar path, I hope my account has helped to comfort and inspire you. Together, we can overcome this disease.

If you have been affected by my story, I would urge you to visit my website below for further information and support.

http://fightback-from-a-brain-tumour.com/.

#fightback

Acknowledgements

Firstly, I want to thank Alison Fenning, a friend and author, for her inspiration and belief in me to write my story as a total novice.

To Nico Dattani, my best buddy, whose wordsmith prowess and dedication got us across the line, we share a common goal to write our first book, over to you now, mate!

Also, I want to thank Graeme Fayers, a friend and talented studio manager, whose teachings in the art of book production did not fall on deaf ears during our car-sharing journeys. He designed the front cover and provided guidance using his vast industry insight on book production.

I want to thank my daughter for her creative talents.

Finally, to my caring and loving wife, my deepest gratitude for her support and input into this book, keeping me honest of my account and memories, and for the tolerance and sacrifice of lost time, while I have been busy producing it.

Praise for Author

"Jason's story was a real inspiration and comfort to me, I thought that if he could cope with such a dreadful period in his life, then so could I!"

- Linda Steward

"Regardless of what happens in our lives, no one is beyond hope, and this is a story of hope and encouragement over adversity. An inspirational story we can all learn something from."

- Gary List

Printed in Great Britain
by Amazon